Suffering

Eternity Makes a Difference

Resources for Changing Lives

A Ministry of
THE CHRISTIAN COUNSELING AND
EDUCATIONAL FOUNDATION
Glenside, Pennsylvania

RCL Ministry Booklets
Susan Lutz, Series Editor

Suffering

Eternity Makes a Difference

Paul David Tripp

P&R PUBLISHING
P.O. BOX 817 • PHILLIPSBURG • NEW JERSEY 08865-0817

Scripture quotations are from the HOLY BIBLE, NEW
INTERNATIONAL VERSION®. NIV®. Copyright ©
1973, 1978, 1984 by International Bible Society. Used
by permission of Zondervan Publishing House. All
rights reserved.

Printed in the United States of America

ISBN 0-87552-684-5

Mary sat across from me, her arms crossed tightly in front of her. "I'm discouraged, angry, and envious," she said. She described how her life had come unraveled as she lost her husband, home, and children through divorce.

Mary came from a good church and knew the Bible. But her situation made no sense to her. "I have no reason to get up in the morning!" She was jealous toward people who seemed to do "whatever they please," yet all went well with their lives.

Most of all she struggled with anger toward God. "How can he say that he loves me?" she cried. "Is this the abundant life he promised? I really thought that he would meet all my needs, but here I am—with nothing! I can't read my Bible, I can't pray, I can't make it through a church service without tears or anger. I look at my life and at the promises of Scripture, and it just doesn't add up! I'm worse off than the average non-Christian."

There is no question that Mary is suffering.

But the way she looks at her life robs Mary (and many like her) of the spiritual resources she needs to face a major trial. She lacks the strength, wisdom, freedom and hope that come from grasping a basic biblical fact: though Christ does not promise to restore Mary to her former way of life, he does promise to restore *her*.

What is wrong with Mary's thinking? I would say she lacks a perspective on eternity. Most people, regardless of their theology, live from day to day without any sense of their eternal destiny. It just doesn't fit the way they think about their lives. But the Bible says that it is impossible to understand what God is doing *or* to face hard times successfully if the reality of eternity is missing from the picture.

If you are a person who is suffering, or trying to help someone who is, learning how to think from an eternal perspective can offer you wisdom and encouragement. Without it, attempts to comfort can fall flat. They seem irrelevant and inadequate, and insensitive to difficult circumstances.

Psalm 73[1] is one place where the Bible teaches us how to look at life from an eternal perspective. Asaph, the writer, describes a familiar experience: we look around and see bad guys prospering and good guys suffering. People who do not know and love God, who in many ways live selfish, arrogant lives, seem to be enjoying lives free of burdens. Meanwhile, believers suffer.

Who of us has not wondered, "What is wrong with this picture?" Is God good to his people? Are his promises reliable? Then how do I understand what is going on around me?

Psalm 73 goes right to the heart of this painful question. It gives us four practical ways to respond to our own difficult circumstances and to encourage others who are struggling to understand theirs.

Step 1: Examine Your Focus (Ps. 73:1–12)

Surely God is good to Israel,
    to those who are pure in heart.
But as for me, my feet had almost
        slipped;
    I had nearly lost my foothold.
For I envied the arrogant
    when I saw the prosperity of the
        wicked.

They have no struggles;
    their bodies are healthy and strong.

They are free from the burdens com-
    mon to man;
  they are not plagued by human ills.
Therefore pride is their necklace;
  they clothe themselves with violence.
From their callous hearts comes iniquity;
  the evil conceits of their minds
    know no limits.
They scoff, and speak with malice;
  in their arrogance they threaten
    oppression.
Their mouths lay claim to heaven,
  and their tongues take possession of
    the earth.
Therefore their people turn to them
  and drink up waters in abundance.
They say, "How can God know?
  Does the Most High have knowledge?"
This is what the wicked are like—
  always carefree, they increase in
    wealth.

Many people measure God's goodness by
their level of personal happiness and their
physical, external, and immediate circumstances. It is hard for them to imagine that
God could be good and not give them their
piece of the "good life."

This is Mary's situation. Her eyes are on personal happiness, and the physical world of the here and now. As long as she focuses on these things, Mary will not understand what God is doing. She will envy the life of the unbeliever and lose her motivation for obedience.

Let's look at three elements in Mary's perspective. Perhaps you will recognize them in your own heart as well.

Created things. Mary tends to define life in terms of possessing and experiencing the things of this world. This goes right to the heart of our struggle with sin. Romans 1:25 says, "They exchanged the truth of God for a lie, and worshiped and served created things rather than the Creator—who is forever praised. Amen."

The key word in this verse is *exchanged.* We exchange God for his creation. Our idea of the abundant life is not to serve God, but to have a happy experience of created things like physical health, friendships, family, financial success, or a sense of emotional well-being.

Asaph struggled with this as he envied the life of the wicked: "They have no struggles, their bodies are healthy and strong. They are

5

free from the burdens common to man; they are not plagued by human ills. . . . This is what the wicked are like—always carefree, they increase in wealth" (Ps. 73:4, 5, 12).

Many people are like Mary and Asaph. They want little more than to be happy—to enjoy a life of relative ease in this world. But if I measure my life this way, God's work will not make any sense. The good things unbelievers enjoy will be a constant source of discouragement.

Present, personal happiness. What is God's purpose for me? Is it to pack my life full of pleasant experiences? What is the "good" that God is doing in my life and the "abundant life" the Bible promises?

Here again, too often we view the purpose and promises of the gospel in terms of our present, personal happiness. We forget that the gospel is more about the coming of Christ's kingdom than our individual enjoyment.

What is God working on? Peter explains, "His divine power has given us everything we need for life and godliness through our knowledge of him who called us by his own glory and goodness. Through these he has given us his very great and precious promises, so that through them you may participate in the divine nature and escape the corruption in the world caused by evil desires" (2 Peter 1:3–4). God's main goal—the chief good he offers us–is to deliver us from our bondage to our own evil desires and to make us participants in his divine nature. He is changing my heart—how I live and what fruit I bear. His focus is eternal and spiritual.

God says that he has given us everything we need to live a godly life. But "everything" does not mean everything we need to fulfill our own definition of happiness. The Bible teaches that God will actually put hindrances in our lives to produce in us the godly character that is his goal (see James 1, 1 Peter 1, and Romans 5). When we conclude that Christians should have greater personal, temporal happiness than the unbeliever, we will have difficulty seeing the good God is doing.

The external, visible world. Christians often compare their pile of belongings with that of unbelievers, assuming that the Christian pile should always be bigger. This surfaced in Mary when her neighbor invited her to a barbecue. There she met this woman's husband, a wonderful guy who related well to his children and helped his wife with the meal. Inside, Mary seethed. Why should this non-Christian lady have such a great man while her husband had been a "monster"?

Many Christians are like Mary, with expectations that leave them unable to cope with life in a fallen world. How different this is from the apostle Paul's reflections on weakness and hardship in 2 Corinthians 4:7–12, 14, 16–18.

> But we have this treasure in jars of clay to show that this all-surpassing power is from God and not from us. We are hard pressed on every side, but not crushed; perplexed, but not in despair; persecuted, but not abandoned; struck down, but not destroyed. We always carry around in our body the death of Jesus, so that the life of Jesus may also be revealed in our body. For we who are alive are always being given over to death for Jesus' sake, so that his life may be revealed in our mortal body. So then, death is at work in us, but life is at work in you. . . . We know that the one who raised the Lord Jesus from the dead will also raise us with Jesus and present us with you in his presence.

. . . Therefore we do not lose heart. Though outwardly we are wasting away, yet inwardly we are being renewed day by day. For our light and momentary troubles are achieving for us an eternal glory that far outweighs them all. So we fix our eyes not on what is seen, but on what is unseen. For what is seen is temporary, but what is unseen is eternal.

Paul focuses on very different things from Mary and Asaph, and it strengthens him to cope with life.

First, Paul focuses on *what God is doing* (v. 7). The weakness, the trials, and the suffering are not some divine mistake, but crucial parts of God's plan.

God wants to draw me away from security in anything but him. So he makes me a weak vessel, to show me that I cannot trust in myself. Then he uses trials to reveal the power of Christ Jesus living in me. As I daily face death, his life is made known.

God is creating eternal changes in my heart, and he will use trials and loss to accomplish this. His goal for me is not the abundance of earthly things, but the abundance of hope in God.

Second, Paul does not focus ("fix his eyes") on what is seen because the *world of physical things is passing away* (vv. 16, 18). One's healthy body grows old. The new house begins to creak with age. We need to build our lives on what truly gives hope.

Third, Paul does not focus on what is seen because of the *reality of eternity* (vv. 17–18). Life viewed from this perspective looks radically different. Though he was beaten, shipwrecked, imprisoned, betrayed, and often ill (see 2 Cor. 11:23–29), Paul describes his troubles as a "light and momentary troubles." How many of us would look at his life and say the same?

Paul saw things this way because he had weighed his troubles against the never-ending glory of eternity, a reality that far outweighs all of these experiences put together.

What a contrast to the way Asaph and Mary looked at life! The difference is focus. Where are your eyes fixed?

How to Examine Your Focus

1. *Understand the power of your interpretations.* Asaph interprets the prosperity of the wicked in a way that plunges him into envy and despair. In a similar way Mary experiences not only what has happened to her; she experiences

her heart's *interpretations* of her circumstances.

Mary said, "I thought that abundant life meant my husband, my children, our house, our family times together, and our church. When all these things were taken away from me, I thought that God had broken his promise and removed what I needed for life. I was left without any reason to go on."

Clearly, Mary was living for the things she treasured. As Christ states in Matthew 6, "where [her] treasure is, there [her] heart will be also" (v. 21), shaping her interpretation of life and thus her response to her circumstances.

If you are in a difficult circumstance, ask yourself: "Where are my eyes fixed? What are the desires, thoughts, and motives of my heart?" Our interpretations are powerful and give shape and meaning to our lives.

2. *Recognize the symptoms of wrong focus.* Psalm 73 points out four symptoms.

First, there is a struggle with envy. Asaph says, "For I envied the arrogant when I saw the prosperity of the wicked" (v. 3). At the barbecue, Mary's assumptions led to bitterness that her neighbor is married to a loving husband and father.

Second, there is a struggle with confusion. Asaph says, "When I tried to understand all this, it was oppressive to me" (v. 16). If I have wrongly concluded that God promises me a trouble-free life, I will think that the wrong people are being blessed.

Third, there is a struggle with discouragement and a lack of motivation for obedience. Asaph says, "Surely in vain have I kept my heart pure; in vain have I washed my hands in innocence" (v. 13).

If I think like Asaph, I lose all motivation to obey God. Personal devotion and prayer evaporate. Attendance at worship services ceases. I withdraw from God's people. This was the case with Mary.

Finally, there is a struggle with anger. Asaph says, "When my heart was grieved and my spirit embittered, I was senseless and ignorant; I was a brute beast before you" (vv. 21, 22). Mary knew all the right things to say about God, but these truths seemed distant from her everyday life. What emerged over time was a deep bitterness and anger towards God.

In her heart she was saying to him, "I have wasted many years of my life seeking to obey you! Give me back my husband and my children because if you don't, your love doesn't mean anything!"

Envy, confusion, discouragement, and

anger are all symptoms of a focus on the created thing. They are windows into your heart.

3. *Identify and confess the true treasures of your heart*. Most people do not deal with issues of the heart. Instead, they talk about the externals, the people and situations that have made them sad, upset, discouraged, or depressed. They think that if these things can be fixed, then they will be happy.

Only when we turn from this external focus to an internal one can we "stand up under" whatever God has ordained for us.

Identifying what is really going on is critical because sin is deceitful. We need others to help us to see our hearts accurately.

Here are some questions that can help you see what you are really living for.

- When do you tend to experience fear, worry, or anxiety?
- When do you struggle with disappointment?
- In what situations do you typically struggle with anger?
- Where do you encounter problems in relationships?
- What situations do you find particularly difficult?

- Whom or what do you regularly seek to avoid?
- What is your definition of a good relationship? What do you expect of others?
- When do you struggle with bitterness?
- How have you struggled with regret, saying, "If only. . ."?
- When do you experience problems with prayer and personal worship, and in your relationship with God?
- When do you struggle with envy?

These questions can help identify the thoughts, motives, and desires of the heart (Prov. 20:5). They make us aware of our true treasures.

Step 2: Examine Your Conclusions (Ps. 73:13–16)

Surely in vain have I kept my heart
      pure;
    in vain have I washed my hands in
      innocence.
All day long I have been plagued;
    I have been punished every morning.
If I had said, "I will speak thus,"
    I would have betrayed your children.

When I tried to understand all this,
it was oppressive to me. . . .

"Conclusions" are the ideas we believe, the assumptions that shape our response to life. Asaph expresses a conclusion in verse 13: "Surely in vain have I kept my heart pure; in vain have I washed my hands in innocence." He is saying, "I wasted my time trying to keep my heart pure. What have I received as a result?"

Mary had a similar theological conclusion that controlled her life. It went this way:

1. If God is good, he will bless the righteous and punish the wicked.
2. God has blessed the wicked while the righteous have suffered.
3. Therefore, God is not good.

Mary's conclusion—based on wrong definitions of "bless" and "punish"—led her to say, "If those people at church had experienced what I have, they wouldn't be so excited about serving God."

People have always found this conclusion attractive. Satan tried to capitalize on it when he said, "If the Lord takes away Job's hedge of blessing, he will curse God" (paraphrased from Job 1:9–11). Most Christians want their service to God to result in a nice spouse and nice kids in a nice house in suburbia. But this is based on a fundamental misunderstanding of what God is doing. He is working on something much grander.

While we focus on good results, God focuses on the process of making us good. We judge his faithfulness on the basis of how many of our desires he has met. But his intent is to free us from our bondage to sinful desires.[2]

Trial and suffering are no indication that God has forsaken his promises. Rather, they demonstrate his unshakable, faithful, redeeming love. He loves us so much that even when we don't "get it," he will continue his work in us until it is complete.

Few people see suffering this way. They find it hard to believe that a good God would plan for us to endure difficulty.[3]

They are shocked by the trials they face and conclude that God must not be who they thought he was. The fact is that he might *not* be who they thought he was—he's *better!* He is after better, eternal things for them than they seek for themselves. Yet their false conclusions lead them to run from God rather than toward him, believing with Asaph that following God is worthless.

We need to understand our functional theology—the conclusions that lead us to do what we do. From there, we can go on to see what the Bible says about them.

How to Examine Your Conclusions

1. *Uncover and evaluate your functional conclusions.* Most people have a view of life shaped by their conclusions about five areas:

- Their past experiences.
- Their present situation.
- Their future prospects.
- Their personal identity.
- God and what he is doing.

If your conclusions are not biblical, there is little hope that you will respond biblically to the situations in which God has placed you.

2. *Learn how to think biblically about your life.* Many people do not use the Bible to make sense out of life. Instead, they use their life experiences to make sense out of the Bible—to dictate what they believe about God, his work, and his Word.

But God's Word is the great interpreter of

life. Its conclusions should determine how I explain my experiences.

To demonstrate this to Mary, I asked her to study Numbers 11, where Israel is in the wilderness, grumbling about manna and crying out for meat. I asked her to identify the conclusions that Moses and the Israelites were making in the five areas mentioned above.

I asked her to identify the kinds of responses that flowed out of those conclusions. This study was eye-opening for Mary. She could see the impact of experiential, unbiblical conclusions and their power to shape our responses. We then applied these insights to her own life.

3. *Recognize and confess where you have blamed God for your disobedience.* Whenever a person who believes that God is in control says, "If only I had_____, then I would be able to_____," he essentially blames God. Such a person is saying that it is impossible to obey God because of the evil he has experienced.

Mary was full of "if onlys." "If only I hadn't grown up in such a driven family," she lamented. "If only God hadn't allowed me to get pregnant so soon. If only I had a loving, understanding husband. If only I had been part of a church that really ministered to my needs."

What is Mary saying underneath? "God, it's your fault. I was ready to obey, but you didn't keep your part of the bargain."

Many people blame God and others for their behavior. But we have already seen that God "has given us everything we need for life and godliness" in Christ (2 Peter 1:3). Suffering does not excuse disobedience or make it acceptable to our consciences.[4]

4. *Face the idolatrous nature of your conclusions.*

A person's tendency to draw wrong conclusions has moral roots. The conclusion that God is not good is rooted in a love for the things of this world and a desire that God would deliver them to us. These desires reveal our patterns of idolatry, which need to be faced, confessed, and forsaken.

James 4:1–10 addresses this issue. James teaches us that human conflict is the result of desires that rule the heart. "You want something but don't get it. . . . When you ask, you do not receive, because you ask with wrong motives, that you may spend what you get on your pleasures. You adulterous people, don't you know that friendship with the world is hatred toward God?"(vv. 2–4). James is saying that the whole idolatrous system of false focus, false interpretations, and false conclusions leaves a person disappointed with life and angry with God. It is rooted in spiritual adultery. Adultery means that you have given love that belongs to one person to someone else.

In Mary's case, she said that she had prayed and prayed, and things had only gotten worse. But it became clear that her prayers were driven by wrong motives, not by a love for God. The more she prayed this way, the more her disappointment and anger grew. Like Asaph, she needed to see the selfish demands that were rooted in her love for the things of this world. These demands put her in opposition to God. Is there a similar problem in your heart?

Step 3: View Life from Eternity's Perspective (Ps. 73:17–24)

. . . I entered the sanctuary of God;
 then I understood their final destiny.
Surely you place them on slippery
 ground;
 you cast them down to ruin.
How suddenly are they destroyed,
 completely swept away by terrors!
As a dream when one awakes,
 so when you arise, O LORD,
 you will despise them as fantasies.

When my heart was grieved
    and my spirit embittered,
I was senseless and ignorant;
    I was a brute beast before you.
Yet I am always with you;
    you hold me by my right hand.
You guide me with your counsel,
    and afterward you will take me into
      glory.

When people typically think about life, they miss the most critical dimension of all: eternity. When I try to bring it up, they often act as if I have quit talking about their life to talk about something distant and unrelated. But discussing eternity is the only way to make sense of the here and now. It is supremely practical.

Psalm 73 takes a dramatic turn in verse 17, as Asaph begins to look at life from this perspective. We see how eternity confronts us with the fact that the created world will pass away. Its permanence is an illusion. Without this perspective the believer looks at his little pile of created goods, compares it to the unbeliever's huge pile, and gets discouraged. How different it is when he realizes that what the wicked have acquired is already fading away, while God has given him an everlasting inheritance!

Asaph uses two metaphors to illustrate this delusion of permanence. First, he says that the ungodly are like people standing on a slippery slope. They may be standing now, but they are going down!

Second, he likens the life of the wicked to a dream. Dreams seem like real life; they are powerful and can leave us shaken. But they are only the fleeting fantasies of sleep.

Such is the prosperity of the unbeliever. It seems so real, so permanent. But it is a flash that will soon be confronted by the lasting realities of life on both sides of eternity.

Many people have an opposite view of life. They *want* the dream, calling the happiness of the here and now the real thing. They are not attracted to the glories of eternity.

This is where Mary was. To her it seemed cruel for me to talk about the unseen love of God or the unseen glories of eternity. She was angry that I would say that God was working on something more wonderful than the loving husband she desired.

But that *is* what God is doing as he expresses his redemptive love for his children. If he is working hard to get us the biggest pile of this world's stuff, he has failed miserably! But why would God waste his creative and redemptive power to give us what is doomed to pass away? Would he be truly good if he did anything less than prepare us for our eternal destiny?

Trials and suffering explode the myth that the goal of life is to get as much as I can. They remind me that the best earthly situations and experiences can pass away, sometimes quite suddenly.

Trials also help me realize who God is and the meaning of the gospel of Christ. Rather than *challenging* the truths of the love and justice of God, trials and suffering *preach* them! It is because of them that God will not let me believe the lie that life is found in the things of this world.

God's love calls me back from hope in the world to hope in him. And in his love he is preparing me for the real thing, eternal glory that far outweighs any pain in this present life. When we understand this, we no longer envy the prosperity of the wicked.

How to View Life from the Perspective of Eternity

1. *Use 1 Corinthians 10:13, 14 to expose the lie that the things of this world are permanent.* Paul anticipates our thoughts in the midst of

difficult circumstances. "No temptation has seized you except what is common to man. And God is faithful; he will not let you be tempted beyond what you can bear. But when you are tempted, he will also provide a way out so that you can stand up under it."

We tend to fear that we have been singled out for particular difficulty. We start believing that God has been unfaithful to us and that our situation is more than we can bear. And we look for ways to escape it.

When Paul goes on to say, "Therefore, my dear friends, flee from idolatry" (v. 14), he is not beginning a new thought (though some translations begin a new paragraph at this point). Rather, he delivers the punch line of the passage! This phrase makes sense of all he has just said.

Why do we question the faithfulness of God? Why do we think we are enduring more than we can bear? Why do we look for any escape we can find? Why are we not comforted by God's presence and promises?

The answer is *idolatry*. Any situation that threatens my heart's desire for the things of this world will seem unbearable to me. God will seem unkind for placing me in that situation, and his presence will offer me little comfort.

At this point 1 Corinthians 10 intersects with Psalm 73. My struggle is not really with what I can endure or with God's faithfulness. My struggle is with my idolatry, which alters the way I think about those things. I grumble and become angry *because* I live for an idol.

First Corinthians 10 helps us see how we have failed to think about our lives from an eternal perspective and what has resulted. It suggests seven questions to ask ourselves:

- How are you tempted to envy others because you felt singled out for a particularly difficult life?
- What situations tempt you to think that God is unfaithful?
- Which circumstances do you think are beyond what you can bear? What things in your life do you think you could not live without?
- What false "ways of escape" do you use to free yourself from unbearable circumstances (such as control, manipulation, escapism, avoidance, and so on)?
- What difficult situations is God calling you to endure right now? What resources has he given you?

- In what things of this world have you placed your hope? What things of this world have kept you going?
- What patterns of idolatry lie at the bottom of these temptations?

2. Recognize, confess, and forsake all discontent, anger, and bitterness toward God that stem from a perspective that forgets eternity. This step was hard for Mary. She found it difficult to admit her anger towards God.

It was a real turning point when she shared, "I was thinking about how difficult it was for me to pray and wondering why. Then I realized that I didn't pray because I was angry with God."

Anger at God is something many people deny. But it must be faced because it reveals the personal agenda that has replaced him.

Step 4: Focus on the Eternal Riches of Redemption (Ps. 73:23–28)

Yet I am always with you;
    you hold me by my right hand.
You guide me with your counsel,
    and afterward you will take me
        into glory.

Whom have I in heaven but you?
   And earth has nothing I desire be-
      sides you.
My flesh and my heart may fail,
   but God is the strength of my heart
   and my portion forever.

Those who are far from you will perish;
   you destroy all who are unfaithful to
      you.
But as for me, it is good to be near God.
   I have made the Sovereign LORD
      my refuge;
   I will tell of all your deeds.

If I am not supposed to focus on the things of this world, what should I think about? The final point of this powerful psalm tells me why I am rich: because of GOD! I am rich not because of circumstances or possessions, but because of the Person who is always with me. His name is Immanuel.

I can look at the wicked and say, "Yes, they have trouble-free circumstances, but I *have* God! I am held by his right hand and guided by his counsel. When my heart fails, he is my strength. He is taking me toward eternal glory. I can look around and honestly say, 'There is nothing on earth I desire besides you. You are my refuge.'"

Psalm 73 confronts us with the amazing realities of redemption. It challenges our belief that we are poor with the reality that we are rich in God. It calls us to the only real hope. Ultimately, it is a powerful warning about distorted perspectives. It demonstrates how our failure to consider eternity can radically alter the way we look at life.

How to Focus on Eternal Riches

1. *Reflect on the practical benefit of God's presence with us.* Biblical case studies on Moses (Exodus 3–4) and Gideon (Judges 6) or studies in Psalm 46 and Isaiah 40–45 can help.

2. *Use God's Word to understand your present experience and shape your response.* Make your biblical interpretations practical and specific. Again and again, ask how the Bible speaks to your difficult circumstances and how it calls you to respond.

3. *Understand your identity in Christ.* Apply biblical truths (especially those found in Romans, Galatians, Ephesians, or Philippians) to the way you understand yourself and your situation. Make a two-column comparison be-

tween how you view yourself and what Scripture declares to be your identity as a child of God.

Conclusion

Psalm 73 reminds us that God seeks to recapture the hearts of his people who have deserted him for idols. He wants them to put their hope in him alone. What does God offer the suffering, discouraged, embittered individual? A set of principles? A way to get the things we want? No, much more and much different.

God offers himself. *He* is our identity, our riches, our strength, our future, and our hope. *He* is what we need. And he is working so that we can say with Habakkuk:

> Though the fig tree does not bud
>   and there are no grapes on the
>   vines,
> though the olive crop fails
>   and the fields produce no food,
> though there are no sheep in the pen
>   and no cattle in the stalls,
> yet I will rejoice in the LORD,
>   I will be joyful in God my Savior.

The Sovereign LORD is my strength;
  he makes my feet like the feet of a
    deer,
  he enables me to go on the heights.
    (3:17–19)

Endnotes

1 Psalm 73 is a *lament*. In great distress the psalmist cries out for God's help; as he does, the confusion, doubt, fear, envy, and anger of his soul are revealed. Psalms like this one bring balance to the way we think about the blessing and prosperity promised us in other Scriptures. They reveal our struggle to understand the mysteries of God's goodness and therefore bring a humble integrity to the way we share his promises with those who suffer. The experience of the believer is not neat and easy blessing. Rather, it is the soul responding to redemptive turmoil lovingly administered by a God who is truly good.

2 See Ephesians 2:1–3; Romans 8:5–17.

3 Psalm 34 can help people struggling with the relationship between the goodness of God and the reality of personal suffering. Here the declaration of God's goodness is placed right next to an account of the troubles of the righteous. The Psalmist does not see suffering as a contradiction to a world ruled by a good God.

4 Since a believer's heart is no longer stone but flesh, he has a sensitive conscience. Therefore, when he sins, either he will place himself, once again, under

the justifying mercy of Christ as he confesses his sin, or he will set up some system of self-justification, such as recasting an event in his mind, blaming someone else, or blaming his circumstances.

David Paul Tripp *directs Changing Lives Ministries for the Christian Counseling and Educational Foundation, Glenside, Pa., where he is a counselor and faculty member.*

RCL Ministry Booklets

A.D.D.: Wandering Minds and Wired Bodies, by Edward T. Welch

Anger: Escaping the Maze, by David Powlison

Angry at God? Bring Him Your Doubts and Questions, by Robert D. Jones

Bad Memories: Getting Past Your Past, by Robert D. Jones

Depression: The Way Up When You Are Down, by Edward T. Welch

Domestic Abuse: How to Help, by David Powlison, Paul David Tripp, and Edward T. Welch

Forgiveness: "I Just Can't Forgive Myself!" by Robert D. Jones

God's Love: Better than Unconditional, by David Powlison

Guidance: Have I Missed God's Best? by James C. Petty

Homosexuality: Speaking the Truth in Love, by Edward T. Welch

"Just One More": When Desires Don't Take No for an Answer, by Edward T. Welch

Marriage: Whose Dream? by Paul David Tripp

Motives: "Why Do I Do the Things I Do?" by Edward T. Welch

OCD: Freedom for the Obsessive-Compulsive, by Michael R. Emlet

Pornography: Slaying the Dragon, by David Powlison

Pre-Engagement: 5 Questions to Ask Yourselves, by David Powlison and John Yenchko

Priorities: Mastering Time Management, by James C. Petty

Procrastination: First Steps to Change, by Walter Hengar

Self-Injury: When Pain Feels Good, by Edward T. Welch

Sexual Sin: Combatting the Drifting and Cheating, by Jeffrey S. Black

Stess: Peace amid Pressure, by David Powlison

Suffering: Eternity Makes a Difference, by Paul David Tripp

Suicide: Understanding and Intervening by Jeffrey S. Black

Teens and Sex: How Should We Teach Them? by Paul David Tripp

Thankfulness: Even When It Hurts, by Susan Lutz

Why Me? Comfort for the Victimized by David Powlison

Worry: Pursuing a Better Path to Peace, by David Powlison